The Whisperings
Of Woden

Galina Krasskova

Other Books by Galina Krasskova

Through New Page Books:
Exploring the Northern Tradition

Through Asphodel Press:
Walking Toward Yggdrasil
Sigdrifa's Prayer: An Exploration and Exegesis
Full Fathom Five: Honoring the Norse Gods and Goddesses of the Sea
Feeding the Flame: A Devotional to Loki and His Family
Root, Stone, and Bone: Honoring Andvari and the Vaettir of Money
    (with Fuensanta Arismendi)

The Whisperings of Woden

Galina Krasskova

Asphodel Press

Hubbardston, Massachusetts

Asphodel Press
12 Simond Hill Road
Hubbardston, MA 01452

The Whisperings of Woden
© 2008 Galina Krasskova
ISBN 978-0-6152-1671-3

Cover Art 2008 © K.C. Hulsman

Printed in cooperation with
Lulu Enterprises, Inc.
860 Aviation Parkway, Suite 300
Morrisville, NC 27560

To Woden and all those who love him.
And to MM, because I promised.

I want to unfold.
Let no place in me hold itself closed,
for where I am closed, I am false.
I want to stay clear in your sight.
−Rainier Maria Rilke

Let the beauty we love, be what we do.
There are hundreds of ways to kneel and kiss the ground.
−Rumi

Acknowledgements

I'd like to offer special thanks to the following people:

K.C. Hulsman for her lovely work in redesigning the cover,

Fuensanta Plaza (Arismendi), Raven Kaldera, Joshua Tenpenny, and the good folk at Cauldron Farm for their collective support (and not just in making this particular devotional possible),

Jess Orlando for her kindness and hard work in proof-reading this manuscript,

and finally Jason Freyson for the gift of his wonderful incense and oil recipes contained in this manuscript.

All errors contained within are entirely my own.

Contents

Foreword to the Second Edition

Three years ago when I first wrote "The Whisperings of Woden," there were no other Heathen or Norse Pagan devotionals on the market. The idea that interiority and contemplative practice, the development of devotional consciousness and the ongoing, mindful opening of oneself to the Gods was something to be valued and consciously sought out was unheard of in the community. It was, in fact, looked upon with suspicion if not downright hostility. Thankfully, this is slowly beginning to change. While ecstatic practices are still looked at askance in the broader community, even within the most orthodox corners of Heathenry, people are starting to discuss and explore the concept of active devotional work. While opinions may vary (heatedly) both on what constitutes devotional practices and what practices are acceptable or acceptably "Heathen," the mere fact that this is now being openly discussed as part of Heathen religious praxis, however tentatively, is a noteworthy change.

This past year alone has seen the publication of several beautiful devotionals, with more in the process of being written. (To date, I can count at least nine devotionals already available.) Two people in the Northeastern community have set up public shrines in their homes (to Freya and Skadhi respectively) where others may go to make offerings. Practices such as the use of prayer beads are slowly becoming more and more popular. Several carved God-posts have been raised in different locales: to Frey, Woden, Gerda, Farbauti, (and there may be more that I'm just not aware of), and the ritual of sacrificial blót, once a mainstay of elder Heathen ritual practice, has once again taken its place as an important and accepted part of modern Heathen and Norse Pagan religious life. This is, quite frankly, remarkable in such a short period of time. It's also something that in my opinion has been and remains desperately needed within the many communities that comprise modern Heathenry and Norse Paganism.

I believe that structured devotional work is very important. The discipline of developing a regular practice, as much as the actual exercises themselves, patterns the mind, heart and spirit of the devotee, instilling a certain receptivity to the Gods. This receptivity and exquisite awareness of the numinous doesn't just happen. It occurs through an ongoing process of spiritual work. Much like developing a physical muscle, one grows into these practices and the spiritual gifts they can bring. A person must be willing, however, to devote time, energy, and awareness to making such acts a regular and important part of one's daily life. While nearly every established religion has a history of such contemplative practices, modern Reconstructionist religions are at a disadvantage in that almost nothing remains in the surviving body of lore detailing anything comparable. Most surviving lore was recorded by Christian scribes who had very little motivation or interest in recording any corpus of Heathen devotional work. It can be difficult to know where to begin. That is the purpose of this book.

Of course, it goes without saying that I hope this book will continue to serve as a useful starting point for those who would like to learn how to deepen their spiritual life. I have made very few changes to the text, primarily correcting a few typos and updating the suggested reading list. I encourage folks to use this book as a stepping stone toward enhancing their own devotional practice and it is my hope that some will perhaps be inspired to write their own devotionals. There are as many ways, after all, to honor and show one's love of the Gods as there are devotees. We must remember that we are not just reconstructing, we are also creating a living, breathing tradition that will hopefully outlast this generation and its descendants. We are, after all, restoring our Gods to active manifestation in the world and that starts with the Midgard of our hearts.

GALINA KRASSKOVA
NOVEMBER 16, 2007
NEW YORK CITY

Introduction

Writing this book has been a difficult undertaking for me. It has both drawn me closer to Odin[1], whom I love beyond breath, while at the same time highlighting the many ways in which I block Him in my life. This project, in fact, began as a meditation on and to Him, a means of reconnecting myself to the God that has been such a powerful part of my life over the past few years. My entire approach to Heathenry has been undoubtedly influenced by my love for the Old Man and it is difficult for me to separate that devotion from my daily, instinctive practice of my faith. Certainly this book is not intended to be a guide to our lore; there are other books that serve that purpose far better than this slim volume. Rather, I hope this book serves as an inspiration to those who may wish to approach our spiritual tradition from a more intimate, experiential level—without losing any of the cultural and religious foundations that a thorough understanding of lore provides. I love our lore. Reading the Eddas, Sagas, maxims, and various historical books has served only to deepen my understanding and love of our Gods. But I love Odin too and sometimes experience goes far beyond the codification of the written word into realms of the heart, realms where the intellect is impotent to define and neatly classify. It is there that trouble often begins for there are no textbooks that even begin to address this path of ecstatic awakening.

Ours is not a religion that has much use for the mystic. For many Heathens, faining or blót is the highest expression of their spirituality and of their devotion to their Gods; and studying the lore the primary means of religious expression. That is fine. But there is another side to that metaphysical coin. Modern day Christian mystic Matthew Fox defines mysticism as active experience of the Divine[2] and postulates that it is the heart and soul of any true spirituality. It is what breathes life,

---

[1] Throughout this book, I freely alternate between several of His names: Odin, Oðinn, Woden. Though some might disagree, I have always believed they are heiti or by-names for the same Divine Being.

[2] "Coming of the Cosmic Christ," Matthew Fox. HarperCollins Press, New York, NY 1988.

inspiration and vitality into our rites and practices just as Odin, Hoenir and Lodhur breathed life, inspiration and warmth into humankind. It is having a conscious sense of the holy, a palpable sense of the permeating presence of the Gods. Over the years, I've come to believe that the highest duty a clergy person has, regardless of faith, is helping people to develop that connection and awareness. I'm sure there are many who will disagree and to them, I say this: to deny the active presence of our Gods all around us and in our lives is to become precisely what the early Christian missionaries accused our ancestors of being: practitioners of useless, dead superstitions. To deny that the Gods may touch us, inspire us, interact with us, becoming *fulltru*[3] in the deepest sense of the word, goes against the very tenets of our lore wherein the Gods were known to walk on Midgard. It is to make of our religion and our sacred traditions little more than an exercise in comparative literature and folklore. And we are so much more than that. Odin is so much more than that.

So this book is, first and foremost, a work of love: love for Woden. In this small volume, I present suggestions and tools that I have found helpful in growing and opening not only to the Gods but to a deeper understanding of lore and Heathen culture. The techniques given are adaptable, and I encourage readers who wish to explore devotional work not to fear experimentation. Devotions of this sort are not to be found in lore. They find their seeds instead in the fertile ground of a heart hungry and aching for connection to the Gods, hungry and aching for that special intimacy that will forever transform one's spiritual life. Devotional work is a tool, one that can assist in sating that terrible spiritual hunger. Of course, such devotional work is difficult to codify and resists the neatly compartmentalized definitions that we have so come to favor as modern Heathens. Dare I say that true experience of the Gods is not to be found only in lore? It takes both the intellectual understanding of our cosmology and our ways and the experiential opening of the heart. Without the latter, our community lacks balance, it lacks vitality, and it will, I believe, ultimately wither and die.

---

[3] Roughly translated: heart friend

This is perhaps best thought of as a book of internal prayer, a mirror that reflects one small facet of the God I long ago fell in love with. Odin courted me and I could not but fall in love with Him; but like any relationship, I found to my surprise that this relationship with a God took work. I am still learning mindfulness, mindful contemplation of Him and of the secrets He has shown me within myself. I hope that this book may help those, who like me, were snatched up by the Wish-Father without warning, those for whom lore is simply not enough. He has become my World-Tree, the axis around which I am centered. I know of no other way to approach Him except through love. And so it is in that love that this book is grounded.

Nine separate devotionals are given here. Some may be done for nine consecutive days, others are ongoing meditations, still others, one-time contemplative activities. The emphasis in each is the development of passionate interiority of practice, the development of what I like to call devotional consciousness. Use them as you will. These meditations are not copied from ancient writings; they come from my own experience and inspiration. They are practices that have helped me maintain a sense of mindfulness and devotion when I was first starting out and to which I occasionally return. They are meant to appeal to all the senses for prayer should, in my opinion, be a full-body experience. Suggestions for further reading and exploration are offered at the end of the book. While going through the various devotionals and meditations, I strongly suggest reading the stories of Odin, books and articles that will enhance one's understanding of the Allfather. Though it is not my primary means of connecting to Odin, I do find that studying them is a meditation in and of itself. There's no need to neglect this. It provides a nice complement to the spiritual work offered here.

GALINA KRASSKOVA
MIDSUMMER 2004

Part 1:

Woden

Woden: Breath-giver

"Thou art my resting-place, my love, my secret peace, my deepest
longing, my highest honor. Thou art a delight of my Godhead, a
comfort of my manhood, a cooling stream for my ardor."
—M. of Magdeburg[4]

He is breath. We are born of His breath. It fills us, cleanses us,
quickens our spirits, awakens us to the holy, that God-Breath within.
Most sacred of gifts, it is His kiss, His caress into being at the
beginning of time. It is what became after worlds collided. With His
breath, He claims us, binds us to being, to conscious acceptance of the
world-gild[5], His pledge. It is an ephemeral cord more binding than the
umbilicus. We are birthed by His exhalation, by the movement of His
lips. It sustains us, seduces us. We feed on it and Him on us, sharing
again and again that birth-bringing kiss.

His breath inspires poets, calls shamans to madness, opens seers to
the bliss beyond time. It sings of sweetness, croons charms of
seduction, whispers secrets beyond knowing, calls the dead to new life.
It shatters the indolent, arouses the hungry, is the sweetest of treasures
to those He is courting. It drives and it goads, cajoles and caresses,
arousing the madness lying dormant within. His madness is ecstasy
born of surrender, rooted in Him as the Tree in the Web. It is the fury
of poets, the passion of mystics, the might of the warrior, raging
berserker caught between worlds. His breath is his magic, forged in
nine songs mighty honed by runes claimed on the Tree. Sweetest of
charmers, this wooer of women, He needs few enchantments to
ensnare the heart. We breathe Him in, imbibe Him with every breath.
Nothing can lock us away from Him, our very human condition craves
His essence. It is the essential component of life.

---

[4] "The Revelations of Mechthild of Magdeburg," or "The Flowing Light of the Godhead," by
Mechthild of Magdeburg, translated by Lucy Menzies. London: Longmans, Green 1953. P. 1.19.
[5] A play on words: wergild is man price, a payment given to forestall blood feud in face of offence,
usually kinslaying.

Odin is the ultimate centering breath, reaching as He does to the very core of our beings, seeing all, gently (and sometimes not so gently) cleansing and opening us, stripping away our various layers of masks and facades. Odin consumes, penetrates, and the seed He leaves in the wake of His passion is the sacred draught of inspiration, the fiery mead which intoxicates only to force its way from the lips of poets and *galdr*-singers. It is the fire of magic, of the weaving of *wyrd*. It gestates in the heart open and yearning for the touch of this God bursting forth in sacred *galdr* resounding throughout the web of being. That is the courting gift Odin leaves in His wake: knowledge of *wyrd* and how to weave it. For if Odin is the breath that sustains life, He is also the lust and passion that fills it, sucking the proverbial marrow out of each and every experience.

Lately when I meditate on the Old Man, it is in His guise as breath-giver that He comes. He is the breath that gives our bodies life: vital, achingly necessary, unseen yet capable of vast devastation if roused. His essence is in the very air that we breathe. Each inhalation becomes an acceptance of a penetration so deep that it occurs on a cellular level; each exhalation a release and surrender to the ecstasy the All-Father is capable of inspiring. He is ardent, enticing, and so overwhelmingly masculine that my own first reaction to Him was to flee. It is one thing to meet Him as Teacher of Runes, to praise Him as Father of Battle, but quite another to find oneself in the midst of an inescapable seduction.

I cannot pinpoint the exact moment my relationship with Him changed. Odin had been a constant in my life for many years but sometime over the past three years, I fell in love with Him in a way far surpassing anything I could ever feel for a mortal man. He snatched me up, courting me always with a smug, wry wit. No one ever warned me that He could be like that. I was completely unprepared. I have often heard the All-Father spoken of in fearful, hushed tones, or with a veiled hostility that is ill served to cover the fear it conceals. I have heard Him spoken of as one who tortures His children for His own ends, who betrays His chosen warriors and drives His women to madness. I have myself experienced the way in which He hones His warriors until they nearly break from the sheer force of the strain. But what I have seldom if ever heard spoken of, except within the small circle of women He has loved, is the tenderness, the fierce protectiveness, the intensity of His passion and the sweetness of His love.

Now, sweet is not a word that one would normally associate with the Master of Fury, Chooser of the Slain! But sweet, caring and tender He most certainly can be. This does not, of course, mean that His challenges cease—on the contrary—but they are balanced by His presence, His caring, and His passion (and above all, this Life Giver to the Gods is a God of immense passion). And whereas it seems He is often antagonistic to His men, He engulfs His women with a desire so intense it leaves little room for anything else. Yet it is a partnership, a synergetic union filled with endless, ecstatic exchange of being, knowledge, and energy. His love is a joy so fierce it burns, a possession so utterly overpowering to the senses that all walls are seared away leaving one as vulnerable, open, and trembling within as a bride on her wedding night. His breath is that of a lover's, deftly revealing our most secret, hidden places, teasing our minds, bodies and spirits to the knife-edge point of metaphysical arousal. He overwhelms.

He has many names this God: Woden, Odhinn (Fury, Frenzy), Allfather, Herjan (Lord), Wunsch (Wish-Giver), Yggr (The Terrible), Veratyr (God of Being), Fimbultyr (Mighty God), Hrjotr (Roarer), Svipall (Changeable), Gangleri (Wanderer), Hangagoth (God of the Hanged), Geirvaldr (Spear Master), Herteit (Glad of War), Glapsvidhr (Seducer), Thekkr (Welcoming One), Sanngetal (Finder of Truth), Oski (Fulfiller of Desire), Sigfathir (Victory Father), Grimnir (Masked One), Bolverk (Bale worker), Harbarthr (Greybeard) to name but a few.[6] Odin as Breath-Giver is tied indisputably with Odin as Father of Runes and Seeker of Knowledge. So many of His *heiti*, His sacred

---

[6] A comprehensive list of His *heiti*, or by-names may be found online at http://www.angelfire.com/on/Wodensharrow/odennamn.html.

names invoke the power of the spoken word, the power of focused breath: Omi (One Whose Voice Resounds), Hvethrungr (Roarer), Vithrimnir (Contrary Screamer), Galdrafathr (Father of Galdr), Gollnir (Shrieker), Eyluthr (Ever-booming) and the list goes on. In magical practice, to speak is to call into being. A large part of rune magic was the chanting of special songs and the singing of runes (called *galdr* meaning "to sing" or "to crow"[7]) to control the unfolding of being. Therefore, to speak is to imbue with life, a power belonging first and foremost to the Gods. In the nineteenth stanza of the *Voluspa*, while speaking of the creation of man, the seeress proclaims:

> *Breath they had not, nor blood nor senses,*
> *Nor language possessed, nor life-hue:*
> *Odhinn gave them breath, Hoenir senses,*
> *Blood and life-hue Lodhur gave.* [8]

Odin as giver of breath may be likened to Odin as progenitor of all, the All-Father, imbuing creation with the animating principle. He breathes life into our most hidden, secret dreams and un-honed talents. He awakens our passions, the fires of inspiration, creativity, and occasionally ferocity within us, and He has the most annoying tendency to throw open doors long thought barred and sealed within the chambers of the heart. More than breath, from the All-Father comes Awareness...a frightening gift at times.

Adam of Bremen in the 11th century declares, "Woden, id est furor." *Woden, He is fury.*[9] Woden is certainly that, but even more so, He is hunger. Throughout the corpus of our lore,[10] it is clear that Odhinn hungers for knowledge. He seeks and even subjects Himself to

---

[7] From the Old Norse verb *gala*, to croak or to crow

[8] *Poetic Edda,* trans. Lee M. Hollander. University of Texas Press. 1962.

[9] *Gods and Myths of Northern Europe*, by H.R. Ellis Davidson. Penguin Books, New York, NY 1964. P. 70.

[10] Modern Heathen primary sources are comprised of the *Elder Edda, Younger Edda*, Icelandic Sagas, Anglo-Saxon Healing Texts, law codes and histories, and current anthropological, archeological and historical analysis.

torture in order to acquire wisdom, knowledge, and understanding. The most notable and well-known example of this is recorded in the Havamal where the All-Father says:

> I know that I hung on a windy tree
> nine long nights,
> wounded with a spear, dedicated to Odin,
> myself to myself,
> on that tree of which no man knows
> from where its roots run.

> No bread did they give me nor a drink from a horn,
> Downwards I peered;
> I took up the runes, screaming I took them,
> Then I fell back from there.[11]

This recounts the tale of how the runes were won: for nine nights of agony, Odin hung on the World Tree Yggdrasil, willingly sacrificing Himself. He hung wounded by his own weapon without food or drink or succor.[12] On the ninth night, the runes surged into His consciousness, He spied them in the abyss beneath the Tree upon which He hung and seized them up triumphant. This one event perhaps most clearly defines Odin's essential nature: the hunger to always go further and deeper. That same hunger often shines forth clearly in those devoted to Him as well.

Certainly this is not the only example in the Eddas of Odhinn's quest for knowledge. We see it again in the *Vafthrudnismal*, where (against the advice of the All-Mother Frigga, I might add), He ventures forth to challenge a wise and cunning giant to a test of riddles. Should He lose, the price would be His head. Of course, Odhinn won

---

[11] *The Poetic Edda*, translated by C. Larrington. Oxford University Press, Oxford, England, 1996. P. 34.

[12] The name of the World-Tree itself means "Steed of the Terrible One", Yggr being a by-name of Odin.

and it was the giant who forfeited his life. Then, of course, we have His winning of the sacred mead, the mead of poetry, inspiration, and creative fire. This mead, Odhroerir, initially belonged to the Gods and was made of their spittle and the ground-up organic parts of the giant Kvasir. It was stolen from Them and eventually ended up in the hands of the Jotun, Suttung. He locked it away in a cave and set his daughter Gunnlod to guard it. Odhinn disguised Himself as Bolverk and won the mead through guile, shapeshifting, and eventually through His seduction of Gunnlod, exchanging three nights of passion for three sips of the mead.

This episode illustrates another of His most outstanding characteristics: the All-Father loves women: all shapes, all sizes, all ages, a fact easily supportable by even the most cursory reading of the Eddas! Take, for example, the *Harbarthsljod*. While Thor boasts of Jotnar He has slain, Odhinn, disguised as Harbard, boasts of His sexual conquests. He cherishes women, most especially those women who cherish Him in return. It can be a shattering experience to truly realize to the depth of one's being the degree to which He loves and cares for His own. My own epiphany came during a *very* intense meditation wherein I was told clearly by the Old Man: "Let this one know that I cherish her broken places. I cherish every rough edge." Simple words but the depth of feeling behind them that I experienced from Him left me utterly shaken and awed. Awed at the enormity of His passion, His love, His caring. Shaken at what that means for me as a woman, shaken at what that means for my own healing.

A word should be said about Odhinn's boasts of sexual conquest. I do not feel that such boasts on the part of a God are ones of betrayal or machismo. Rather, they are an admission of a sexuality, energy, and vital force too powerful to be contained; of life and exuberance, of strength, above all, of vitality, of seizing the moment in a life that is all the sweeter because it must seem so fragile, so threatened to those Gods whose ears are constantly straining for the blast of Heimdall's horn. And for every person who opens to Him, who loves Him just a little, who is able to contain for however short a time, a single drop of the enormity of His essence, more of Him is able to be in the world. We are doorways, vessels, windows for this most active of Gods.

Perhaps it is not surprising for a God so strongly associated with vital power that we also find in Woden a God of healing, though this aspect of His nature was strongly suppressed during the Christian conversion of Scandinavia and Iceland. To my knowledge there are only three extant sources citing Odin as healer. The first one is the Second Merseburg Charm in which an injured horse is healed by being "charmed by Wodan, as well he knew how...":

> "Phol and Wodan rode into the woods,
> There Balder's foal sprained its foot.
> It was charmed by Sinthgunt, her sister Sunna;
> It was charmed by Frija, her sister Volla;
> It was charmed by Wodan, as he well knew how:
> Bone-sprain, like blood-sprain,
> Like limb-sprain:
> Bone to bone, blood to blood;
> Limb to limb—like they were glued."[13]

The second instance is the *Song of the Nine Sacred Herbs from* the Anglo-Saxon *Lacnunga* manuscript which says:

> "...then Woden took up nine glory-rods, / struck the adder then so it flew apart into nine, / there apple ended it and its poison / so that it would never bend into a house. / Chervil and fennel, two of great might, / the wise lord shaped these plants / while he was hanging, holy in the heavens / he set them and sent them into the seven worlds / for poor and for wealthy, as a cure for all."[14]

---

[13] Translated by D.L. Ashliman, Ph.D.: http://www.pitt.edu/~dash/ashliman.html
[14] *The Lacnunga Manuscript* quoted from *Leechcraft* by Stephen Pollington. Anglo-Saxon Books, Trowbridge, England, 2000. P. 217.

The third instance is the second rune charm from the Havamal wherein He speaks of runes one must know if one wishes to be a healer:

> "*I know a second which the sons of men need, those who want to live as physicians.*"[15]

I have no doubt about His healing power, though, and have experienced His care when I was ill and injured. I've felt Him holding me when I have cried in pain, experienced Him walking me home, supporting me when I fell ill at work (to the point I fully believe to the depth of my being that He was visible to other passersby) though I myself felt only the sense of strong support. I have had Him guide my hands in rune working and whisper sage counsel in my ear as I minister to my students and clients. Certainly, He has effected my own healing in heart and spirit. He opens, He overwhelms, but also, He restores, and that is something all too often overlooked in favor of His battle-wisdom. I find sustenance in both.

Of course, Woden also has His darker side. He is cunning and implacable, fierce and brilliant in battle. He leads a host of the dead in the Wild Hunt and He possesses the power to command the dead to do His bidding.[16] Many of His *heiti* speak of His ability in combat: Herblindi (Host Blinder), Hnikudr (Overthrower), Valgautr (Slaughter God) and of His fury: Thror (Inciter of Strife), Woden (Fury), Vidurr (Killer) to name but a few.[17] He is an Ordeal Master, subjecting Himself to agonizing ordeals to win power, wisdom or knowledge and occasionally demanding of His devotees that they do the same. He is a Wanderer, wandering endlessly throughout the worlds in search of knowledge, of wisdom, of some craft to hold Ragnarokk at bay and perhaps to increase His own knowledge-hoard. There is great comfort, however, in knowing that here is a God who will treasure a warrior

---

[15] *The Poetic Edda*, translated by C. Larrington. Oxford University Press, Oxford, England, 1996. P. 35.

[16] Such as when He summons the seeress forth in the Voluspa and commands her to scry the future for Him.

[17] *Gods of the North* by Brian Branston. Thames and Hudson Press, NY, NY, 1980. P.112.

spirit. Here is a God who finds strength and vicious cunning, love of battle and willingness to fight as intoxicating as a woman's beauty or sweetness of spirit. There are times where He may be fierce and harsh and demanding of those He claims, but how He also cherishes them. I have experienced Him as filled with an immense grief at how wounded and scarred His children can be. Part of loving Him, at least from my own experience, has been to shoulder and share a small part of that grief.

Being an Odin's woman, for me, has rapidly come to mean creating a place of welcome and comfort for this God. His presence is constantly palpable; I have only to reach out to feel His strength engulfing me. That constant presence has taken on some surprising and heart-warming manifestations in the last few years. He has become a partner in my life and home, a companion in the most unexpected of ways. It is difficult for me to speak of the Old Man solely from the context of myth, though I certainly enjoy reading of His exploits. I can speak of Him only as I myself have experienced Him: as Lover, Teacher and Beloved Friend. I wear His symbol on my skin, the *valknot* (three inter-locking triangles symbolizing at the most basic level, that its bearer is dedicated to Odin, a sacrifice to Odin to be claimed at will) with immense pride as a wife would wear a wedding ring or a queen her crown, for it marks me as belonging to my Beloved. It is a symbol of my bond with Him and all that entails.

In the next part of this book, you will find meditations, devotionals, and activities that over the years I have come to delight in. It is my pleasure to share them now. They are simple, most of them very tactile, but they have served to aid me in maintaining mindfulness in my daily life, in my devotional discipline, and in the way in which I stand in relation to my Gods. I know of only one way to approach the Old Man, and that is from the heart. It is in that spirit that these meditations are offered.

Part 2:

The Devotionals

All-Father,
I ask for Your blessings.
Breathe into me,
Oh God of gainful council.
Nourish me, Wish-Giver,
that I might know You more fully and well.
I hail You, God of wisdom, cunning and inspiration.
Wondrous Healer, Nourisher, Welcome One,
Be welcome in my life, my home, my heart.
Master of the Tree, I sacrifice to You:
My fears, my doubt, my hesitation.
Breathe into me. Open me, Wisest Lord.
I will seek You with the fervor
with which You sought the runes.
Be my mead, be my joy,
be the prize at the end of my seeking.
Hail, Woden, All-Father,
Wondrous Lord.

The First Devotional:
The Ritual Bath

To the modern Heathen mind, devotional practices such as those about to be described might seem strange and unusual. Yet some of them, like the idea of a cleansing bath, are drawn from folk practices in Germany. Others, such as the box meditation, are modern inspirations. At the heart of these practices, however unusual they may seem, is the goal of drawing closer to the Gods, in this case Odin.[18] They create a sense of continuity of practice, of daily mindfulness that is often difficult to attain in our modern world. Personally, I have drawn great nourishment from ongoing meditations such as these.

The following cleansing bath may be done for nine consecutive days. It is a process of symbolically washing oneself with All Father's *wod*.[19] I have created it out of herbs and scents that I personally associate with Woden.[20]The bath is fairly simple to make, though it does take a bit of preparation.

Bring ½ gallon of water to a boil. Add the following:

- 1 cup of yew needles
- 2 cups of oakmoss
- 1 cup of ground myrrh
- 2 cups of sandalwood
- cups fresh red rose petals
- 1 cup deerstongue
- 1 cup lavender

Right after boiling, add:
- ½ cup of musk oil
- 1 cup of rose water

---

[18] Each of these devotionals, with the possible exception of the ninth rune-based devotional, can be adapted for use with other Gods or Goddesses.

[19] Personal energy and force. It is etymologically linked with the name Woden.

[20] A full list of Wodinic herbs is given in the Appendix.

- 9 drops of rose oil
- 9 drops sandalwood oil.

Boil 10 minutes, then allow the blend to cool completely. Strain out the herbs and flower petals. Strain into bottles and store for nine nights in a dark place before use. When you are ready to actually take the bath, begin by lighting a white or blue candle by the bathtub (blue is a color often associated with the Old Man). Then take the cleansing bath while doing one of two things:

Add two cups of the Odin Bath to the bath water and soak for 10-15 minutes, making sure to submerge every part of the body including the top of your head. Take a regular bath, then stand and pour a cup of the Odin Bath mixture over your head and body. (In many folk traditions, such as hoodoo, this is the preferred way to take a cleansing bath. I personally prefer the first though.) Allow it to dry on the skin and then dress in clean clothes. This method is excellent if one only has access to a shower.

Go back to your altar, if you have one, or your bedroom, and put a few drops of Odin oil[21] in a bowl of water. Offer the water to Odin and rub that between your palms and over your body right over your clothes.

Burn a bit of the Odin Incense[22] (this incense can be burned on small, self igniting charcoal that can be purchased at any occult store), or a cigar, and cleanse yourself with the smoke. This is called smudging, smoking or recaning[23]. After cleansing yourself with the smoke, smudge the entire room. At this point, you may wish to meditate on Woden, talk to Him, or even spend a bit of time reading and meditating on His lore.

This completes the first devotional.

---

[21] See Appendix

[22] See Appendix

[23] Native American practices and Wicca both utilize smudging extensively; however, there are also records of *recels* being burnt for ritual/healing purposes in the Anglo-Saxon healing manuscripts.

I will hail the bold God, Lord of Asgard's Hosts.
I will praise the Lord of Valhalla.
I will celebrate His strength, cunning, and wisdom,
this God of warriors and kings.
I will praise Him, the Allfather,
Husband of Frigga, Delight of Her arms.
I will hail the Drighten and Ring-giver,
Whose gifts inspire His chosen.
I will laud this Wooer of women,
Whisperer of charms and seduction.
I will sing of the Master of Poets,
Ensnarer of many an unwary heart.
I will raise a horn in His honor.
May victory be Yours, Valfathr.
Hail, Woden! Hail the Wisest of Counselors!

The Second Devotional:
Creating a Devotional Altar

I have always delighted in altar work. For years, it has been my favorite meditation. It soothes my spirit and delights both eye and heart in a way that no other contemplative art can. My altars have grown to encompass nearly every room in my house, from the tall ancestral altar right inside my front door to the long main altar in my ritual room to my small personal altar dedicated to Woden: the first thing I see upon waking, the last upon retiring at night. My altar has always been a point of surety for me, a touchstone in the midst of spiritual storms. It reflects my spirit and without it, I am unsettled within. I need that spiritual canvas upon which to work. The creation of an altar is an act of birth, of transformation, of giving life. It is the physical counterpart to the spiritual garden that the true devotee tills and nurtures within the soul. The altar becomes the focal point for the spirit, a place of peace and healing where one's connection to the Gods is celebrated and nourished, a place where spiritual strength is revitalized. It is a place of peace and of dynamic internal transformation.

In this devotional, the objective is the creation of a personal altar. This creation is a very intimate act, for an altar speaks to us in symbols, and symbolism is the language of the spirit. It is the language with which the Gods are able to circumvent and outwit our analytical, stubborn and often cynical mental censors. It combines the visual with the kinetic and reaches out to the child within enticing us to exploration and play. It opens doors of the spirit and its form is limited only by the imagination of its creator. Each altar is different just as every person is different. Everyone comes to the Gods in their own time and in their own way. One's personal altar is an expression of that often circuitous and challenging journey. There is power in symbols, and the sublime often lies hidden in the simplest of talismans. That is something that I believe Odhinn learned when He hung for the runes, a thing shamans have always known. Symbols speak to the heart as nothing else can. Altars evoke the power of our spirits by calling forth those symbols we most cherish. It puts a face on the experience of the sacred, on where we allow the Gods to reach and where we most block Their touch.

Creating an altar, no matter how small, not only reverences Divinity and provides a focal point for meditations and prayers, but is also beautifully symbolic of the centering of one's life around the Gods. It becomes a place where one may return again and again to center oneself, to pray, to meditate and to listen to the Divine reply. It is symbolic of an open heart and mind, a welcoming spirit, a soul ready to enter into a love affair with the Gods.

The creation of a personal altar is the creation of sacred space, a seat of honor for the Gods and Goddesses—a throne, if you will, for the pleasure of Deity. It is an act of hospitality and welcoming. An altar isn't simply a convenient space upon which to randomly throw ritual tools; it is a living, changing, magical offering to the Gods. It is a thing of beauty, of creation, representing in palpable physical form all those things symbolic of the heart and its journey. One is "laying a foundation in truth...laying a foundation in the heart."[24] from which further creation may burst forth. It has been my experience that an altar perfectly reflects where a person is at in faith, in life, in balance. An altar will change as one grows and matures for it is the seat of one's spiritual power, a living, changing nexus of transformation. It is important to remember that creation never reaches stasis but is always an ever-balancing rhythm between order and chaos, harmony and evolution.

In ancient Egyptian theology, the soul is seen as being composed of nine separate parts, each of which interacts with and affects the other soul-bodies around it. The most corporeal of these is the *khat*, an ancient word meaning "the fire altar".[25] The *khat* was the actual physical body, the flesh, that which was consigned to earth as the heart and mind and will were consigned to heaven. It was the sacred ground, the place wherein the burnt offering was made, an offering of the self. It is that which contains the seed of transformation, like the physical

---

[24] "Dreams of Isis," Ellis, Normandi. Quest Books, 1997
[25] "Dreams of Isis," Ellis, Normandi. Quest Books, 1997.

altar, the place where transformation and growth may occur. It is the temple of the spirit, and just as the *khat* is the container of the soul's vibrant, ever-changing energy, so is the altar its physical, earthly counterpart. As above, so below, and always ever-renewing. It is through the *khat* that one's soul may touch others, and it is through the contemplation of the Gods and Goddesses, the first step of which is often the construction of an altar that one may be touched with the illumination of Divinity. The *khat* is the conductor through which the soul speaks and moves; the altar is the nexus around which Divine power gathers. One becomes the microcosm of the other.

In Heathen theology, the soul also has many parts. There is the *lík* (physical body), the *önd* (divine breath of life), *hamingja* (luck), *maegen* (vital force), *willa* (will), *hugr* (intellect), *mynd* (memory), *odr* (passion/ecstasy/inspiration), *fylgja* (guardian spirit), *orlog* (personal wyrd), *hamr* (etheric soul skin), and *mod* (self-consciousness...the part of the soul incarnated in the here and now—which presupposes that other incarnations are held separately within this soul matrix as well). The *lík,* like the Khemetic *khat,* is the container of our vital essence, the vehicle by which we are able to actively manifest our will, desire, and inspiration upon the physical world. It is also the tool by which we are able to interact with the Gods through the filter of the physical. Our bodies form a very important bridge, one that makes sacred the physical while at the same time making (to some degree at least) concretely knowable the spiritual. This is, to my mind, profound ... and the altar is a microcosm of that.

The altar is a living prayer, a call to the Gods to come into our lives and hearts. Like an open door, it welcomes consciously the touch of the Gods, the transformation, the immolation, the rebirth. The altar is the desire and devotion of the soul made form. When the Gods descend, the altar becomes the throne upon which They sit. It is a place of constant work, constant change, constant devotion, and like a seed planted in the earth, it is only through tender care that it may blossom into a rich garden of passionate living faith. The altar is the beginning. It is the foundation, like the earth upon which we rest. It is the living flame of our faith, a beacon of and for the Gods. The greatest altar is that of the spirit which we carry within our hearts, but it is only through caring cultivation both within and without that the inner flame may burn its brightest.

So create an altar to Woden. There is no limit or rule to what can be placed on an altar. Craft it of those things that most remind you of this God. If you possess images of Woden, such things make excellent center pieces for an altar, but if not by all means improvise. Make it yours, a thing unique to you and the way in which you interact with the Old Man. Once you have created it, using those things that call to mind the sacred to you personally, commit to spending a few moments in quiet contemplation in front of your altar nightly. This can make all the difference in laying the pattern of a mindful spiritual practice.

This completes the second devotional meditation.

You are there in my hunger.
You evoke the greatest need.
Devour me, Herjan, in my longing.
Pierce me and penetrate
with the spear You bear so proudly.
Cast it through me
and set me to war
against all that would separate me from You.
Be in me.
And hold me in Your heart,
my Lord.

The Third Devotional:
The Sacred Feast

Offering food and drink to our Gods is a staple of Heathen worship. It's also a powerful opportunity to meditate on how deeply the Gods can nourish us and what we ourselves have the chance to give back in return. A connection to the Gods shouldn't be something to be endured (as I have often heard said by certain Heathens), it should be something to be celebrated, cherished and reciprocated. Offering food and drink and other gifts to our Gods is a very palpable way of demonstrating and honoring this mutual bond. We can be self-reliant and in love with our Gods at the same time.

The meditation tonight is a fairly active one: cooking and offering a sacral feast to Woden. Each person should feel free to improvise and offer what he or she feels is appropriate. I can only suggest what I myself have found fitting. In the second night of our devotional practice, we created a personal altar to the Old Man. Here, we continue that meditation. I keep the food out for 24 hours and then dispose of it, usually by taking it out and laying it beneath a yew or ash tree. Some folks might be uncomfortable with the apparent waste of the food, and if that's the case, cook the food and share it with Heathen friends or family, offering it first to Odin.[26] Sharing the meal by oneself with the Old Man can also be a valuable meditational experience. Those who have never cooked before should give it a try. It's really not as difficult as you may think.

Suggestions for food offerings include:

- pot roast with vegetables
- smoked salmon
- aquavit

---

[26] I do not consider it a waste of food to leave food out for the Gods or ancestors, even if the food is only going into the trash after a set period of time—corporeality being no set indicator of existence where Gods and ancestors are concerned! By feeding Them/them, we are establishing a bond of reciprocity and affection. We are welcoming Them/them into our homes, hearts and families.

- mead (there are several commercial brands available which, while not as nice as home-made mead, are perfectly acceptable substitutes)
- apple pie
- fried apples with sweet sauce
- Icelandic black bread
- Havarti cheese
- Gjetost cheese
- bean soup
- spice pie
- cinnamon pudding
- stuffed fish
- orange-glazed beets
- dark chocolate
- marzipan

The purpose of this meditation is to consider how we are nourished by the Gods, and how we *allow* Them to nourish us, and what we are willing to give in return. To begin with, choose a drink that you really, really like. It doesn't have to be alcoholic but it does have to be something you absolutely enjoy. Either set up the following at your altar or on the table where the feast is laid out (provided it is to be shared only between you and Woden).

Once you have your altar (or table) set up, set out five small glasses arranged in a circle with a sixth and bigger glass in the center dedicated to the Old Man. Fill the five smaller glasses to the brim with the liquid of your choice. The circle of glasses represents:

- Relationships (friends and family)
- Spiritual devotion
- Career and financial stability
- Romance and sex
- Health and well-being

With each of the smaller glasses, meditate on how much of that particular aspect of your life you *cannot* give up. Drink that much from the glass. That is what you are saying "I need." After you've done that with all five glasses, pour the remaining liquid into the center glass. This is what you are saying you can give to Woden. Now, spend some time really thinking about the results.

Really think about how deeply connected you are (or are not) to the Old Man in the various areas of your life. Think about how and where you block Him and why. Sincerely think about how and where you would like to be more open to Him and ask for His help. Woden isn't going to take everything away from you. You're asking Him to help you give more (hence open to Him more) and thereby provide a greater opportunity for Him to return the gift, giving to you in exchange. This is a meditation on Gebo in action.

This meditation represents an ongoing process and should be done every few months. You can see how the glasses change and how your relationship with Odin has been and is manifesting in your life. Leave the glasses up on your altar for 24 hours and then dispose of them by pouring the contents outside.

This completes the third devotional meditation.

Odhinn, breathe into me.
Strengthen this warrior's heart.
Nourish these fighter's hands.
Open me, to all that you are.
My heart is hungry for Your spear.
Breathe into me,
my Beloved.

The Fourth Devotional:
Valknot Centering Meditation

The *Valknot* is specifically a symbol of those dedicated to Odin. In fact, it is often referred to as the Knot of Odin. It is formed by a series of three triangles overlaying and interlocking with each other.

It is both an extremely powerful symbol and an extremely mystical one. On one level, it represents one who is dedicated to Odin, to be used and claimed as and when He sees fit. I've heard many Heathens wryly describe it as the "insert spear here" mark. Many people devoted to the Old Man eventually end up having this tattooed on their body. One of the most intriguing speculations on this modern custom is that it is a way of distinguishing Odin's people on the field of battle: spiritual or physical, so that when the Valkyries come to claim us, They will know that we are bound for Valhalla.

On another level, it represents both the wound of Odin's spear, where He blooded Himself upon the tree and the shaman's ability to journey between the worlds. It can also be representative of spiritual, mental, emotional and temporal wholeness. Of course, by its number three, it is a reminder of the nine days and nights of Odin's seeking on the Tree. The *valknot* is a symbol both of His sacrifice and of our goal and journey. It makes an excellent visual mandala on which to meditate, though it is a complex one. I have found that mentally tracing the pattern in the mind's eye makes it far easier to visualize.

In order to do this meditation, you will need to know the seven primary chakras and their locations. Working with these points is an excellent means of centering oneself and unblocking constricted energy. It's not in our lore, but it is a useful adaptation for meditational work, and some Heathens might argue that we share a common Indo-European connection with Hinduism and other Eastern religions. Be that as it may, these are useful focal points for this meditation, so I have chosen to use them. I am also personally attached to this meditation as it was the very first one I ever learned.

In this meditation, we start with the upper-most chakra, the crown chakra, and work down. One can, however, just as easily reverse this process.[27]

The Chakras

There are seven main chakras in the body and they can impact one's emotional health and/or create blockages that can impact one's spiritual journey. Therefore, it is necessary to keep them clean and well balanced. Below is a chart giving some correspondences for each of the chakras. This may help in your work with them.

For those who are devoted to Odin, the following meditation may be used utilizing the valknot symbol. It may also be done with a rune—Ansuz is a good choice for this type of work because it clears away blockages. Other runes can, of course, be used as well.

---

[27] A colleague once told me that men often find it easier to work from the crown downward and women from the root upward, but your mileage may vary.

Chakra	Location	Color[28]	What it governs	Element
Root Chakra	Perineum	Red	Survival, material support, health	Earth
Sex Chakra	3" below the navel	Orange	Desire, self image, self confidence	Water
Solar Plexus Chakra	Below the breastbone	Yellow	Self-mastery, will, motivation	Fire
Heart Chakra	Center of the chest	Green, or pink	Emotions, love, loss, ompassion	Air
Throat Chakra	Bottom of the Neck	Blue	Expression, communication	Sound
Third Eye Chakra	Between the brows	Indigo or white	Magic and psychic gifts	Ki (Chi)
Crown Chakra	Crown of the head	Purple	Wisdom, Divine connection	Divinity

---

[28] I have given the color correspondences as I myself first learned them. In authentic Tantric practice, the color correspondences may vary significantly.

The Meditation

To begin, find a comfortable position, close your eyes, and begin to focus on the rhythm of your breathing. It's usually best to do this type of meditation sitting up, otherwise as you become more and more relaxed you might find yourself falling asleep! (I have a relaxation exercise in which you begin at the toes and slowly relax every muscle group until you reach your head. By the time I reach my ankles, I'm out like a light!) Spend a few moments concentrating on the sound and rhythm of your breath. Odin owns breath and this is His essence, His *odr* filling you. With every inhalation, be consciously mindful of that Divine energy filling every part of your body from the tips of your toes to the crown of your head. With each exhalation, consciously release all tension, stress, and all that may block that Divine *odr*. This can be a complete meditation in and of itself: starting at the tips of your toes, with each inhalation feel every part of you being filled with Odin's breath. It is like a kiss, you are sharing the same breath, breathing in that life-giving *odr* from His mouth to yours. Continue focusing on His breath until you feel the vessel of your body overflowing with it, until it bursts forth from your crown and that power flows down around you.

Some of you may choose to stop there. For those that wish to continue, once you have reached the state where you are thoroughly encompassed in the breath of Odin and you are comfortable and relaxed, with your mind's eye, focus on a point about two feet above your head. Now some people are very visual, others kinetic. If it is easier for you to *feel* the energy rather than see it, that's OK. I'm like that for the most part. Do whatever works best for you. The language of meditations tends to be written in very visual terms, but it's perfectly OK to adapt this for kinetic or non-visual people and there's nothing wrong with doing so. Those whose primary learning/processing modality is auditory may benefit from either chanting Odin's name as the *valknot* penetrates each chakra, or actually chanting or singing runes instead of a *valknot*. Either way, the unconscious mind responds quite powerfully to such guided meditations as this one. They are extremely useful tools in developing an awareness of the Divine presence. So focus on a point two feet above your head and see or feel a blazing white-blue *valknot* shining there. It radiates and pulses with energy.

Feel or see (or both) a shaft of pure blue-white light containing the form of the *valknot* (or whatever symbol you have chosen) descending to pierce your crown chakra. Once the *valknot* penetrates your crown chakra, it becomes a vibrant royal purple. Feel that light glowing and pulsing within your chakra, opening it (traditionally, chakras should be around three inches in diameter), and cleansing it, removing any blockages or constraint.

Once you are satisfied that the crown chakra has been thoroughly cleansed, feel that *valknot* moving to the third eye. Here, it becomes a deep indigo (if this color is too difficult to visualize—which it was for me for a long time—go ahead and visualize or feel pure white light). Once this chakra has been thoroughly cleansed and opened, continue to the next. Repeat this process through to the root chakra. The color of the valknot changes as it enters each chakra, glowing blue for the throat, green for the heart, yellow for the solar plexus, orange for the navel and red for the root. Take as much time as you need with this part of the meditation.

When the root has been thoroughly cleansed, visualize a thick cord extending from the root deep into the earth. Exhale and feel the *valknot* leaving your body through the root chakra and descending into the ground beneath you. It remains connected to your root through this glowing golden cord and as it penetrates the earth, its energies branch out into a thick, solid, interlocking network of roots like the foundation of some ancient tree. Feel it moving down through the floor, through the foundations of your apartment or home and into the land beneath you.

As you inhale, draw energy in from the *valknot* that glows above your head. Feel it flowing down the now opened chakras and as you exhale send that energy deep into the earth. Continue this process for a few minutes, feeling the energy branch out, traveling along the system of roots you have created, rooting you deeper and deeper to the earth. Once you are feeling well and truly grounded, extend those roots to touch the core of the earth, be conscious of its molten center and begin to draw that primal, vital energy up through your root chakra, through all the open chakras you have just cleansed, and send it up into the *valknot* shining from the heavens above your head.

Continue this for a few moments, then attempt to both send energy down from the *valknot* above your head and draw energy up from the earth so that you have a balanced, continuous flow. It helps to alternate breaths, grounding for one breath cycle, and drawing energy up for one breath cycle. Don't worry if you can't quite manage this, it takes time to master.

I like to end the meditation by focusing first on the grounding pattern, sending all extra energy down into the earth, but some people prefer the revitalizing feeling left from pulling in primal earth energies. Do whatever works best for you. When you are ready, begin to focus only on your breathing again and slowly return your consciousness to temporal time and space. Some people become slightly lightheaded after meditations. If this is the case for you, spend a few moments focusing on your breath thusly: inhale four counts, exhale six counts, hold six counts for 5-10 minutes in a repetitive pattern. As you do so, see/feel all of the excess energy in your body sinking into the earth. This breathing pattern automatically grounds most people.

If you are choosing to do this particular meditation for nine consecutive nights, one may choose to use Ansuz for its opening properties rather than a *valknot*. The *valknot* is generally seen by those devoted to Woden (and a large majority of American Heathens) as a symbol marking its wearer as lawful prey for the Old Man, one He can claim whenever and wherever He wishes. Unless one has this type of relationship with Him already, using the *valknot* in this meditation can be quite intense and may bring one closer to Odin than initially expected.

This completes the fourth devotional meditation.

May I be broken.
May Your force press into me beyond my ability to contain.
May I be driven, an exile into Your arms.
May I be given nowhere else to turn but to You.
May I be broken open like ripened fruit
and raised to Your lips, Oh God.

The Fifth Devotional:
Creating an Odinic Reliquary Box

This is actually one of my favorite meditations. Not only does it appeal both visually and kinetically, but you end up with a lovely meditation piece that can be used on the altar for future devotionals. Perhaps it just appeals to the child in me; I always did like to secret my treasures away! Regardless, this is very similar to creating a medicine bundle; you are creating a focus for future meditations, a reservoir of feeling, concentration, and energy.

Begin by selecting a wooden box. It can be as simple or as elaborate as you like. In the box, place items that you *personally* associate with Woden. I'll give you an idea of what I have in my own meditation box, but keep in mind, this should be taken as a guide, not an exact list of what must go in the box. Contents will be different for every person who creates one of these boxes.

Suggested ingredients:
- A pouch of Woden's nine sacred herbs (see Appendix I)
- Several small yew twigs
- A pouch of meditation stones. These were a gift from a friend. She chose stones that had words such as "warrior", "north", "prayer", "silence", "truth", "balance" – things she associated with our kindred. They are in a rich royal blue velvet pouch.
- An Ansuz pendant on a blue cord
- A *valknot* pendant
- Several chunks of labradorite (I personally associate this stone with Him in my personal devotions.)
- A lapis ring
- A silver ring with runes
- A set of runes on blue tiles
- Raven feathers (They were gifted to me by a friend who found them upstate.)
- A vial of Odin oil

- A phallic-shaped piece of jalap
- Nine dried roses from a special Odin ritual
- An amber necklace
- Labradorite prayer beads
- Several pieces of turquoise
- A cross stone
- A *valknot* pin
- A chunk of dragonsblood
- Several crystals
- A runic pendant with one of the starburst sigils from Stephen Flowers' *Galdrabok*
- A pendant with an image of Odin on it
- Clove cigarettes
- Several prayers written out on pretty paper
- A small heart shaped stone
- A handful of ash leaves
- A small spear-shaped pendant
- Wolf fur
- A pouch of Odin incense (See Appendix I)
- A small eagle carved out of bone
- An eye patch
- A small gandr[29] with runes carved on it
- A small knife
- A small bottle of whiskey
- A cigar
- A small pipe
- A pouch of tobacco

This provides some idea of what might go into these boxes. The important thing is not to limit yourself to this list alone. Be as creative and as personal as you possibly can be. Don't worry that you might forget something—you can always add new ingredients later. Like an altar, the contents of this box will grow, change, and evolve as you

---

[29] wand

reach new levels of understanding in your relationship with Odin. Lay the contents out on your altar. Smudge the box and all the contents with Odin incense and begin to talk to the Old Man. Offer each item to Him, explaining why you are adding it to the box. Does talking to Odin on such a simple, personal level sound surprising? This is exactly the type of personal relationship that it is possible to develop with our Gods. Even in our lore, They were often referred to as "fulltrui"—heart friends. Just as with any other relationship, good heart-felt conversation is an essential foundation. Once the box has been completed, close it and ask Odin to bless it, to impart a bit of His *odr* to it, that it might serve as a symbol of His presence and power. Then place it on your altar for future contemplation.

This completes the fifth devotional.

Where You wander, I will follow.
When You are weary, I will be your comfort.
When You hunger, I shall be Your sustenance.
Devour me, Whisperer of secrets.
You are the beating of my heart,
the rise and fall of my breath.
You are the pulse of my very life's blood.
You are all that entices, all that ensnares.
Envelop me, Gangleri.
You are the shattering silence,
in which I hear Your cry.
You are the encompassing darkness,
in which I am burned by Your light.
You are the sturdy roots of the Tree,
and I, its blossoming fruit.
You are the blade, and I the sheath.
You are the spear, and I the wound.
You are the hunter, and I the prey.
You are the fire, and I am the wood.
You are the rider, and I the willing steed;
You are the fertile earth, and I am the seed.
Yours is the hunger, mine the need.
Pierce me, Odhinn.

The Sixth Devotional:
Writing as a Meditation

Just as the study of sacred texts can be a valuable devotional experience, so can writing. Any exercise of our creativity has the potential to bring us closer to the Gods. This is a sacred channel, one with not only the power to open and transform us but with the twin potential to touch and transform others. It is a very, very powerful thing. Many of the ritual tools that we may study and practice have the side effect of helping to unlock one's creative processes. I personally never realized how important this was for truly healthy spirituality until I happened to stumble on a book called *The Artist's Way* by Julia Cameron. The entire premise of this delightful book is that we are all creative people. All of us have an "artist within" that needs to be nurtured in order for us to be sane, whole, and healthy. Much of this sentiment is echoed, albeit in far more theologically astute terms, in the writings of Creation Spirituality proponent Matthew Fox. It boils down to one thing: creativity is a channel to the Divine. It benefits us on all levels: spiritual, emotional, mental, physical equally. Perhaps this is why Odin went to such lengths to acquire the mead of inspiration.

Studying the sacred stories can provide an unconscious impetus for the deepening of our spiritual practice. The stories found in the Eddas provide a roadmap to greater comprehension of the nature and wisdom of our Gods. They give us the symbols and language with which to share and express the hard-won epiphanies. This is not to be underestimated. The very act of sharing often encourages greater spiritual exploration in others. It is as though a subconscious floodgate is opened. There is a certain reciprocity in the entire process of spiritual emergence.

One thing I have discovered in ten years as a priest is this: learning to really communicate on an open, unselfconscious level with the Gods can be damned difficult. I've struggled with it at times and I've seen just about every person I've ever taught, counseled, or shared ritual with struggle with it, sometimes wrenchingly so. Sometimes it is simply difficulty with emotional intimacy, sometimes it is an unconscious carry-over from the Christian idea of a judgmental, harsh, remote God, or there may be a number of other reasons. Many people find that communicating through the written word: journals, praise poems, prayers, even letters to be far easier (especially in the beginning) than communicating aloud.

This night's meditation is comprised of several parts: a journal meditation, a letter and the writing of your own personal prayer. I would suggest beginning the preparatory cleansing bath at dusk to give yourself plenty of time for this devotional. The important thing is to relax, take your time, and don't judge your written results too harshly. This is meant to be an offering of the heart, mind, and creative spirit.

Before you reach this point in the nightly meditations, you'll want to select a special journal. Most large bookstores or stationary stores carry a selection of blank journals. Take some time and choose one that appeals to you as a meditational tool in your work with Woden. Choose one that appeals to your sense of beauty and creativity. It's easier to maintain an ongoing process of journal work if you actually like the book that you're writing in! Your tools should, whenever possible, be aesthetically pleasing as well as functional.

Part I

After your daily prayer and cleansing bath, take your journal and begin by writing out your own spiritual history. What brought you to Heathenry? What were the major influences in your spiritual life? What moves you? What motivates you? Why do you want to grow closer to Woden? For the first entry, relying only on your own inner voice and your own personal wisdom, assess your own spirit. What do you perceive as your soul's strengths and weaknesses? What are your talents? What are your vices? What is your perception of Deity and your concept of your relationship to Deity? Write down what you believe to be positive and negative influences upon your spirit. Write down people who have been instrumental in guiding or offering sound advice to your spirit thus far. Peek and poke into every corner of your inner landscape. What are your dreams, your aspirations, your fears? Write down everything you feel would paint a true picture of your spirit. (This may take more than one night. Begin with this night's meditation but continue this writing process for as long as you need to, even if it takes several weeks).

After you are through with this exercise, interpret and envision all the data expressed in this first entry as a tree. Draw this tree, naming the roots, the soil, the trunk, the branches, the leaves, the flowers, and the fruits which symbolically represent an insight explored in the first entry. Do not neglect to include influences like the sun, rain, and lightening which strike down your tree. Maybe birds or other animals live in your soul tree. Take as much time as necessary to draw a complete and accurate image of this tree and name all the parts of the scene as completely as you can. The tree can be one of your own design or of a specific real species you are particularly drawn to. If you discover a major idea in your first entry that you cannot seem to fit anywhere in the tree scene, write it somewhere in the air of the scene and circle it to meditate upon later.

All other entries in this Spirit Journal will directly relate to the first entry or the tree drawing. As you do the various exercises to commune with Woden and to get you on the road to your spiritual path, be conscious of any wisdom, thoughts, or sudden insights you may receive on your tree or first entry. Write it out, noting any changes to your original thinking that may have occurred. (This is something that you may wish to return to every few weeks or months as you gain more insight into your spiritual evolution.) If the labeling on the tree needs to be changed, write the entry out in your Journal as a gardener's direction or observation, i.e.: "leaf or branch named _____ needs to be pruned" or "root named _____ is unhealthy" or "flower named _____ is the most fragrant." Write down how your relationship to your own spirit is evolving. Write down new gifts you discover and name them as parts of your tree. Do the same with new influential people you may encounter. This is your own personal record of the spiritual advancement of your own soul focusing on your spirit.

Additionally, keep a second journal. This second journal is your "Journal of the Journeying." The Journal of the Journeying should focus on the voice and influence of the Gods and contain all of Their wisdom you have received. Invocations and prayers should be written in the Journal of the Journeying. Entries suitable for a diary should be written in your Spirit Journal. Try to write an entry in your Spirit Journal at least once a week, two or three times during particularly inspirational moments. All that you learn, are now, and will become should eventually be a part of this Spirit Journal.

Part II

Once you have finished part I of the journal meditation, write a letter to Woden. Be as open and honest with Him as you would a close friend that you hadn't spoken to in a long time. Approach Him with the utter openness of a child if possible. No one is ever going to see this but you and the Old Man, so try not to feel self-conscious or shy. If you can, write it out on nice stationary, seal it up and take it outside and bury it under a favored tree. Think of this as a sharing of the self with Woden. Nothing is more important than nurturing that bond. Nothing should ever take precedence over developing that relationship. Opening fully to the experience of the Divine can be fraught with many challenges, however, not the least of which is our own internal resistance to the inevitable process of surrender. The majority of ritual work is designed to bring about that surrender, that melting into the arms of the Divine. During this process we also learn a new way to see: slowly but surely we begin to recognize the touch of the Gods in our lives, to recognize the patterns, rhythms, and symbols that make up the warp and weft of existence—the very things that we have been taught in our society to disregard and ignore. And those very things that we fight so furiously against are the very things that our souls crave the most.

It is a terrifying task that one is asked to embark upon: without having directly experienced the immense ecstasy of Divine "Isness," one is asked to undergo a spiritual journey that will upset and restructure his or her entire life, to face emotions long buried and to relearn an emotional skill-set that is sorely lacking in our world today. It is daunting and it is in this process that one's kindred and one's teachers are of utmost support and importance, for all of us have gone, at some point into those darkest places within. By working through the ritual process, we are essentially making a terrifying leap of faith and trust.

Part III

The final part of the writing meditation involves writing your own prayer to Woden. Though (hopefully) as we go along, we all learn how to write the traditional hails and bedes, it's important to develop your own personal style of communication and prayer as well.30 I don't believe there is any right or wrong way to pray so long as it is true and from the heart. It's amazing how many Pagans and Heathens dismiss the idea of prayer as a Christian convention. It is not. The earliest known prayers were recorded by a Sumerian priestess named Enhenduanna. They are beautiful paeans of praise to the Goddess Inanna, ecstatic hymns celebrating Her sovereignty over Her people. They strongly influenced the writing of the biblical Song of Songs. Certainly scores of ancient Egyptian prayers exist for everything from praise to healing to simple gratitude. There are even surviving prayers amongst the Norse, found most notably in the Sigdrifumal of the Poetic Edda and in Gisli's Saga. Clearly, the Christians did not corner the market on prayer! I do, however, find great spiritual nourishment in the writings of the Christian Rhine mystics—women who had an ecstatic relationship with their God and who were often looked upon with suspicion if not outright persecution by their Church. I cry when I read the prayers of Mechthild of Magdeburg (one of the Rhine mystics who lived in 13th century Germany). She speaks of her God as her lover, as palpable a lover as any mortal man could ever be, and there is such joy and such longing there that everything in my soul cries out "Yes, this mirrors my love for Odin." I have found in the writings of

---

[30] 'Bede' is an Anglo-Saxon word for 'prayer.'

this long-dead woman a kindred spirit, one that nourishes and nurtures my own often painful spiritual openings. Sometimes the strength of my prayers and the knowledge that others too have found it a similarly painful journey are the only things that keep me from faltering and falling. It is a lifeline, often agonizing but always there.

In fact, I think that's the most important thing about prayer: it strengthens and nourishes our connection to the Gods. Sometimes though, I think the entire act of praying really opens up a proverbial can of worms! I have been praying to Odin recently to teach me to love better. All of a sudden, every relationship that I cherished in my life began to fall apart. I find that all the places where I block that flow, that give and take of energy and emotion, caring and affection are suddenly highlighted. Suddenly, I am given opportunity after opportunity to directly address those areas where I am lacking in trust. Thank you, Odin ... I think. I have been given great conflict in answer to my prayer. The ball has been tossed into my court, so to speak. A path of action has been pointed out to me where only confusion and inaction existed before. This brings up one very important aspect of prayer: it does not, in any way abrogate one's personal responsibility. Nor does it rob us of our personal power. It enhances, compliments, and empowers.

So close this night's writing meditation with your own prayer. It can be as elaborate or as simple as you wish, but make it yours and make it an utterance from the heart.

This completes the sixth devotional meditation.

Woden, You are in all the dark places
I so desperately seek to hide.
You have traced each of my scars within
and cherish them.
You have seduced me, Terrible One
and willingly, I allow You to steal my breath,
replacing it instead with nine drops of sacred mead
bestowed by kiss upon my parched lips:
Ecstasy, madness, inspiration
Truth, terror, shattering beauty,
Sacrifice, longing, and need.
I do not fear You,
not even when you burn beneath my skin,
when we share the cloak of flesh together.
Instead, I will glory in You,
I will celebrate the fury You bring.
I will feast on *wod*, as on the finest wine.

The Seventh Devotional:
Ritual Anointing

Prior to doing this particular meditation, make up a bottle of the Woden oil.[31] This oil should ideally have a chance to blend thoroughly, and I personally prefer to let it sit for several weeks, though there is no reason it cannot be used right away. (Keep in mind, however, that the scent will change the longer the oils are given to blend.) A nice meditation might be to make up the oil before beginning the first devotional in this book and then let it sit and blend until you reach this, the seventh devotional.

Begin by sitting before your altar and focusing on your breath. This meditation is really an activity, but it begins with a centering prayer. As you breathe, focus on Woden's name. Inhale and mentally pray: "Woden, Allfather..." As you exhale mentally say: "Open me." Continue this for ten to fifteen minutes. Not only is this a centering and focusing meditation, but by slowing your breathing, it has the effect of putting one in a very grounded, relaxed state. My little mantra may be replaced by inhaling and exhaling while repeating several of His praise names or any Woden-centric mantra of your choice. Instead of praying mentally, it is perfectly acceptable to sing or chant or say the prayer aloud as you breathe.

After your centering prayer, take the vial of oil and cup it in your palms. Ask Woden to bless it and fill it with His *odr*. Then take a bit of the oil between your hands, rub it between your palms and perform the following self-blessing:

I am filled with *wod*. I embrace it.

I stand centered in Woden. His ecstasy flows through me, bringing wisdom and inspiration.

---

[31] See the Appendix

(Anoint your head) I am the faithful friend of Woden. His sacred breath fills my crown. It illuminates. It opens. May I always be connected to His Divine presence. Hail, Woden.

(Anoint your forehead) I am the faithful friend of Woden. His sacred breath, which is wod, fills my mind. It brings clarity and dispels darkness. May I be mindful of His Presence in all things. Hail, Woden.

(Anoint your lips and throat) I am the faithful friend of Woden. My mouth and throat are filled with His sacred breath. Wod flows from my lips. May I always be conscious of the power of my words to harm or to heal. Hail, Woden.

(Anoint your heart) I am the faithful friend of Woden. My heart is filled with His sacred breath. May it overflow with the furious ecstasy of His presence. May my heart always remain open to Him. Hail, Woden.

(Anoint your stomach) I am the faithful friend of Woden. My stomach is filled with his healing breath. He sustains me. He renews my spirit. May I ever be nourished by His Presence. Hail, Woden.

(Anoint your back) I am the faithful friend of Woden. My spine is filled with His sacred breath. It is strong, as the Tree is strong. It provides unending support. May He ever remain my strength and my foundation. Hail, Woden.

(Anoint your genitals) I am the faithful friend of Woden. My genitals[32] are filled with His sacred breath. Through them, my hunger is His to feast upon. Through them, may I celebrate my passion and creativity. Hail, Woden.

(Anoint your legs) I am the faithful friend of Woden. My legs are filled with His healing breath. They carry me wherever He would have me go. May I ever journey safely under His care. Hail Woden.

(Anoint your feet) I am the faithful friend of Woden. My feet are filled with His mighty breath. I walk surely, confidently, not fleeing my sacred duty. Each step brings me closer to Him. Hail, Woden.

(Anoint your hands) I am the faithful friend of Woden. My hands are filled with His sacred breath. Through them, He touches Midgard. May my actions and work ever be pleasing to Him. Hail, Woden.

My blood is filled with *wod*, my breath is Woden's breath. I am His living sanctuary. I am His faithful friend. Hail, Woden.

Spend a few moments contemplating the meaning of the blessing, contemplating what it means to be so strongly open to the All-Father. When you are ready, offer thanks to Woden.

This completes the seventh devotional meditation.

---

[32] Feel free to substitute whatever word you prefer to use in referring to your genitals.

Weapons-brilliant, Battle Lord,
I praise you.
In my heart, You stand triumphant.
You have vanquished me,
and rendered me Yours.
You stand victorious
in a battle wherein no weapons
were raised.
I will praise you, Mighty Warlord,
and cherish Your tenderness
With me, your fallen prey.

The Eighth Devotional:
Travelling to the Tree

There is a definite art to guided meditations and pathworkings. They develop a very special type of focus and concentration, and through stretching the muscles of the creative imagination they enable us to unconsciously give the Gods openings that They may otherwise not have. Not everyone will respond well to such techniques. It took me years before I was able to gain any benefit from guided meditations. Folks who are primarily visual will usually do very, very well with them. For those whose primary learning modality is auditory, recording and playing back this type of meditation can be particularly efficacious. Those who are kinetic may need to expend a bit more time before they see the same type of results. But it is a worthwhile endeavor.

The secret to doing a good guided meditation is to take it slowly. The meditation given below is a framework, an outline. It isn't something that is meant to be read verbatim; rather, it provides the basic outline from which one can expand and journey forth. Sometimes, one will end up travelling on a completely different mental path, and the existing framework will be abandoned, serving as nothing more than a starting point. That is perfectly all right. Don't be afraid to experiment and let your imagination roam freely. Sometimes, I have found, the Gods inspire us through dreams, creative inspiration, and pathworkings. It is not something to disregard lightly.

I would also suggest doing such meditations in a sitting position. I have found that folks tend to fall asleep if they meditate lying down. This happens because when we meditate, we relax. This is a positive thing, but if one is exhausted, it is a precarious line between relaxation and sleep. Though I may use the term "visualize" in the meditation below, there are many ways to do this. Those more kinetic in learning orientation may find it easier to feel the journey unfolding before them and through that, gain a type of creative vision. Use whatever sensory method works best for you.

Pathworking

Begin by finding a comfortable seated position and closing your eyes. Focus on your breath. With each exhalation, allow all the tension in your body to dissipate. Feel the rhythm of your breath flowing through you, soothing you, carrying your attention away from the world around you. Continue this until you are completely relaxed. Do not rush; this is a very centering meditation in and of itself.

Once you are ready, keeping your eyes closed, visualize yourself in an open field. Before you there is a path continuing as far as the eye can see. Take note of what the field looks like, the flora and fauna, the sky, the light, scents, and textures. Begin to follow the path. Take your time, observing everything unfolding around you. This path will lead you to a huge tree: *the* Tree, Yggdrasil. It is immense, rising above you further than your eyes can follow, its thick, gnarled roots digging deeply into the earth beneath your feet. Its wood is rough and textured and some find symbols of power etched into the bark. To some, it is a specific tree; to others, an indeterminate genus. Others find it a blend of every Tree. Regardless, it is impressive, awe-inspiring, majestic. This is a holy place, a powerful place. The air itself holds a unique charge. Take your time and examine the Tree, touching it as you will.

Walk around the body of the Tree until you find a crevasse, a hole, an entrance of some sort. Perhaps it will be hidden amongst the roots, perhaps it will be in the body of the tree itself, or perhaps it will be in the earth, unattached to the Tree. Once you have found your doorway, and you will know it for it is unique to you, enter it. Be cognizant of any animals that may serve as your guide. Go through the door, whatever it may be and follow it until you come to a sacred place, within the body of the Tree.

Take a seat on one of the gnarled roots, or on a stone, or any place that you find comfortable. Within the Tree is much as without, and there are branches with leaves twining about the cavern. A single rune burns on each of the leaves. Collect three of them. Runes are one of the means by which the Gods may communicate with us. Look at the first leaf. This represents everything that blocks your spirituality, all the obstacles and challenges to your creative inspiration, goals, and spiritual evolution. Think about what this rune represents, how it plays out in your life, and its long-term impact. Take up the second leaf. This represents where you need to be, the most positive unfolding of your wyrd. Overturn the third leaf. This rune will give you the tools to make that journey. Note well the runes and any other omens that may be evident. Omens are portents written in the natural world. It is possible that you may be visited by ancestors, *disir*,[33] even Odin Himself. The mental state created by such meditative work provides the perfect psychological opening for such visitors to utilize.

Remain in this place for as long as you desire. When you are ready to depart, retrace your steps until you have exited the doorway and stand again in that place before the Tree. As you look around, you spy the path that led you to the Tree. Begin to follow it again, back from whence you came. With each step, begin to focus on your breath. With each breath, you become more and more aware of your physical body, of the room around you, of the temperature and textures, sounds and scents. Continue focusing on your breathing until you feel yourself fully grounded. When you are ready, open your eyes.

It is advisable to take some time to write down the results of your meditation. This place within the Tree may be returned to again and again in private path-workings.

This completes the eighth devotional meditation.

---

[33] Protective female ancestors

I sat beneath the burning tree
And the wind whispered
Songs of anguish,
Breaking
Bowing
Till bloodied lips the earth embraced
Consumed in fire
From fire born
Within to without
Heart plunged into the fires of God
No bonds need hold me
Though my spirit shrieks aloud
From the searing kiss of
that scorching love.
Let my flesh be burned
By Love
Beneath the Tree
Where Love sacrificed itself
for me.
Give me burning.

The Ninth Devotional:
Crafting the Runes

Necessary tools for this meditation:

- Blank rune tiles
- A dremel or carving implement
- Odin incense
- Odin oil
- Odin's nine herb tincture and loose combination of herbs
- Soil
- Tobacco (a cigar is perfect)
- A diabetic sticker
- Mead or red wine

(All incense and oil recipes are available in the Appendix.)

Tonight's meditation is quintessentially Odinnic. It involves crafting a set of runes and empowering them to be a tool of communication between you and the Old Man. The runes can be used for further meditation with Woden; in fact, I suggest meditating for 24 consecutive nights—one rune per night, writing your own rune poem for each rune as you meditate. The winning of the runes is such a powerful part of Odin's story that it seems only fitting to include it in any devotions to Him. Though most often the runes are presented as tools of divination or magic, they are also very potent tools of contemplation, meditation, and connection to the God of the Tree. In fact, this is often overlooked in light of their other uses.

In creating your own set of rune tiles tonight, we will be focusing on furthering your communication with Odin. Regardless of whether the runes are used in meditation or for the reading and untangling of *wyrd*, they are tools of enhanced communication. They are keys that open doors of clarity and understanding. We will approach them as semi-living tools, hard won and greatly treasured by the All-Father.

Making your own set of runes is not as difficult or as daunting as it may sound. The first step is to select your wood, cut the tiles to size, and sand them. I'm no artisan so I tend to go the simple route; I purchase blank tiles.[34] You can choose from a selection of woods though, of course, I recommend the yew or ash. Some folks may choose to use river stones and carve the rune into the stone (I've known a few people who did this and though time consuming and difficult, the results were most rewarding) and others may wish to make their runes out of clay or some other natural substance. There are a number of options available. Those more gifted in craftsmanship than myself may choose to cut and sand the wood themselves. If you choose to cut your own runes, please be respectful of the Tree and leave an offering for the *vaettir* when you take the necessary branch for your work.

Once you have chosen your wood and cut (or purchased) your rune tiles, set them out on your altar and smudge them with Odin incense. As He breathed life into humankind at the beginning of the world, we are asking Him to breathe life into these blank tiles, which will soon become runes. The next step is to carve or burn the runes into each of the tiles. You have two choices here: you can use a Dremel tool to burn the shape of each rune, or you can carve the rune into the wood. Both a Dremel tool and a basic set of carving tools (which I strongly suggest over and above a knife, though I suppose a knife would work too) can be purchased at almost any art supply shop.

Take your time with this step. Read up on each individual rune. I've suggested a few useful titles at the end of this section. Meditate on it, not only on the traditional meaning but what it means for you personally, how it has played out in your life, how it has the capacity to connect you to Woden. Examine the rune tile carefully to see where the rune is best placed upon it. Lightly sketch the rune with a pencil and then either burn or carve its shape upon the wood. Once you have finished, sing the rune name three times. (This is a form of *galdr*.) Continue until you have completed the Futhark.

---

[34] I recommend http://tarahill.com/runesets.html for blank tiles.

Throughout this series of devotional meditations, I have consistently emphasized the importance of singing prayers, chanting runes, vocalizing one's intentions. This is a very important part not only of rune work, but also of claiming one's creative power. Odin is a God of inspiration and communication, and there is much to be gained by delving deeply into such vocal practices. It may be uncomfortable at first, but learning to confidently use one's voice to call the Gods or invoke a rune is one of the most powerful and spiritually healing acts a person can perform. It is yet another conduit by which one can connect to Woden's presence and power.

Once you have carved or burned the runes into the wooden tiles, begin the process of empowering them. Like any living thing, they must be fed and given purpose. The first thing that we want to do is blood them. After this step, the rest is simplicity itself! Rune workers and occultists would say (and rightly so) that by sharing your blood with the runes you are creating a connection between them and yourself, as well as symbolically sacrificing as Odin did during his ordeal on the Tree. It is a quid pro quo deal. It goes without saying that one should *never* share a cutting implement. Blooding the runes is a personal act, it's not something that should be done with others anyway, but be safe. Use common sense. Now, I usually use a small, sharp knife but most folks will probably find it easier to use a diabetic sticker. (When I use a knife, I cut my fingers. Never ever cut the wrist or arm, you run the risk of slicing open an artery.) Taking up each rune, starting with Fehu, smear a few drops of blood on the rune and intone its name again. Do this until you have completed the entire Futhark. Be sure to put hydrogen peroxide or antiseptic cream on your finger. (I study sword work and have far too much experience with cutting my hands. The smallest of cuts can lead to the nastiest of infections. Use the antibacterial cream even for just a pinprick. Better to be safe than sorry.)

Next, take up the runes again and anoint each one with the following substances, galdring its name as you do so. In order, anoint the runes with: blood, Odin oil, Odin incense, your own sexual fluids, nine herbs tincture, loose nine herbs mixture, mugwort (for vision) and tobacco and/or blueing. After each anointing and *galdr*, ask Odin to imbue these runes as living things with His essence that they may be effective tools of communication between the two of you. You want a tool that will grant insight into every aspect of your life and that will provide clear, accurate communication. By anointing the runes in the way described, you are giving of yourself and also helping to imbue them with Woden's energy. This may seem rather esoteric for the average Heathen, but I believe it to be a worthwhile meditation nonetheless.

If you are doing just this particular meditation for a span of nine days, it can be broken down thusly:

- Night one: carve the runes
- Night two: blood the runes
- Night three: anoint with oil
- Night four: anoint with incense
- Night five: anoint with sexual fluids
- Night six : anoint with nine herbs tincture
- Night seven: anoint with nine herbs
- Night eight: anoint with soil
- Night nine: anoint with tobacco

Before each anointing, meditate on the rune as discussed above. After each anointing, *galdr* the rune and pray to Odin. Once all this is done, put the runes in a pouch or box of your choice and handle them in the following manner:

For three nights, leave them on your Woden altar. You can carry them with you during the day. Anoint them w/oil or smudge them with incense but do not yet try to read with them.

Sleep with them under your pillow for one night.

Leave them on your ancestral altar for three nights asking your ancestors to bless them and lend their own might to this tool of communication.

Sleep with them under your pillow.

Bury them in the earth for three nights.

Sleep with them under your pillow.

Now you have a rune set that you can be proud of. You will grow stronger in your ability to use them as you practice, and at the very least, you have a worthy gift for Woden.

If you have a rune set already that you absolutely love, you can still do this meditation using your current set. Simply omit the carving/burning part of the process. While some runic purists will insist that one *must* make one's own set from scratch, I do not hold that particular view, and I find that properly blessing and empowering a pre-made set to be nearly if not as effective.

Offer a glass of wine or mead to Woden, and spend however long you wish meditating on His quest for the runes.

This completes the final devotional meditation.

Epilogue

I have come to the conclusion, after many years, that those who love Woden are conduits for Him, open doors through which He is able to experience the world and through which we are able to experience Him. I hope it is not mere hubris, but I would like to think that part of my purpose is to do that for Him. Woden can be harsh in the manner in which He drives His own, but I have never, ever experienced Him as cruel. It was He who first taught me the ecstasy of prayer, of the conscious co-mingling of my spirit and His, taking me far beyond what I had ever thought prayer could be. I wrote earlier that when Adam of Bremen wrote "Woden, id est furor" that he missed the point, or perhaps grasped only one small facet of this God's nature. He isn't fury but rather pure ecstasy of spirit, heart, and mind; the ecstasy that propels the soul into greater and deeper being. I do not know how one could experience, truly feel His presence and not love Him, not fall in love with Him.

There are many, many ways of honoring the Gods through personal devotional practices. The meditations and activities given in this book represent only a few, the ones that personally appeal to me. They are no substitute for prayer and simply spending time in the presence of one's Gods. They augment and complement an ongoing devotional life. Daily contemplation, reading sacred texts, faining well—all of these things contribute to a healthy spiritual life. Woden, as I have known Him, has become my spiritual center. I hope that this book reflects that, conveying a little of the God that I have come to love these past few years. If it has done that, then I am content.

This fulfills a promise I made to Woden last Yule. It is my gift to Him.

Agonistic Exchange in the Body of a God

Before I ever read Rumi,
I prayed for burning.
Before I ever read Mechthild
I knew what it was to dance in Your storm.
Before I ever knew
The bite of the blade that is Your love
I ached for it.

They warned me loving You would bring pain
A thousand voices doubled and tripled in their cries:
His touch is anguish, betrayal and suffering beyond measure.
Beware. Be warned. Flee. But do not call His name.
Do not rush like a hapless leaf
Carried on the buoyant wind into His arms.
Do not do this thing
That will surely shatter you forever.
Please...
Those voices begged.
I did not listen.
I sought You out:
You, my dead and deathless God,
A walking corpse,
A creature of hunger,
Cold fire imprisoned in the taut, sinewy vessel of flesh.

It is said that Gods are creatures of spirit alone,
With no flesh to captivate the senses,
With no cast of skin and bone and taut, heated muscle
By which a thousand passions are known.
But I have tasted You.
I have felt Your hands: hard, calloused and rough
Pressing me back against the Tree,

Where passion had its way once with You.
I have writhed in sweetest anguish
Calling only Your name, Odin,
As You drove Yourself beneath my skin,
Heedless of my cries, my terror,
The ecstasy strung like shimmering beads of dew
On a spiders web between each gasping moan.

I loved a man once,
Even through the inferno of Your affections.
I love that man still.
Yet when You are there,
I cannot see Him through the fury
That is Your presence.
I am in love
With the monstrous paradox
Of You.

You steal my breath,
Each exhalation captured in Your waiting mouth
A war of conquest upon my soul.
Oh my Hunger, You devour my life,
Drop by savored drop.
I am fermenting in Your hands
Against Your lips.
I have no more words.
I cannot write about anything
Save how You have plundered my world,
Oh my God.

Appendix

Recipes

Odhinn Devotional Oil

> ½ oz each: oakmoss oil, myrrh oil, sandalwood oil, rose oil
> ¼ oz ambergris oil (a synthetic is fine)
> One piece of galangal stored in the oil jar.

> If you are using an oil to cut this blend, use sweet almond oil.

Odhinn Incense #1

Mix the following oils/essences on black woodbase:

- Ambergris resin
- Ambergris oil
- Vanilla essence
- Bayberry essence
- Soak dried clover flowers in musk oil.
- Soak oakmoss in oakmoss oil

(Allow both the woodbase and clover and oakmoss to dry completely before adding the following herbs:)

- Mandrake
- Deerstongue
- Spikenard
- Dragonsblood
- Star anise
- Balm of Gilead
- Cedar
- Hyssop
- Lemon balm
- Mistletoe
- Oak

Mix all in roughly equal parts. Allow Odhinn to guide you in this.

Woden Incense #2

- 7 tablespoons of red sandalwood
- 3 ½ tablespoons of frankincense tears
- 1 ½-2 tablespoons cinnamon
- 1-2 tablespoons cedar
- 2 tablespoons finely chopped oakmoss
- 1 ½ tablespoons crumbled ash leaves
- 1 ½ tablespoons spikenard
- 1 – 1 ½ tablespoons mistletoe
- 1 tablespoon chamomile
- 1 tablespoon rosemary
- 1 tablespoon deerstongue
- 9 drops fig oil
- 9 drops amber oil
- 9 drops bergamot oil

Grind and blend thoroughly together. This should, ideally, sit for nine weeks in a dark place before being used. The scent changes dramatically the longer the ingredients are allowed to blend. It should be stored in glass. The oils can seep into plastic or wood containers.

Herbs Associated With Woden

(Some of these herbs are associated with Woden in folklore; others come from modern Heathens who worship Him. The herbs marked with an asterisk are from the Song of the Nine Sacred Herbs. Opinions vary on whether to use Belladonna or Viper's Bugloss.)

Ash
Basil
Belladonna*
Bergamot
Betony
Cedar
Celery
Chamomile*
Chervil*
Cinquefoil
Crabapple*
Dandelion
Deertongue
Eyebright
Fennel*
Fly Agaric
Frankincense
Galangal

Horehound
Jalap
Lavender
Mugwort*
Nasturtium
Nettles*
Parsley
Periwinkle
Plantain
Rose
Spikenard
Vanilla
Viper's Bugloss*
Walnut
Yellow Dock
Yew
Yohimbe

A combination of any nine of these makes an excellent Woden-centric cleansing bath.

Suggested Reading

(I have included not only books about Woden, but also devotionals to other Norse Gods, as well as a few basic books of lore. Several novels are included as they present interesting and surprisingly accurate portraits of the Old Man.)

Bauschatz, Paul, (1982). *The Well and the Tree.* MA: The University of Massachusetts Press.

Bellows, Adams, (1926). *Poetic Edda.* London: America Scandinavian Foundation, London.

Branston, Brian, (1980). *Gods of the North.* NY: Thames and Hudson.

Branston, Brian, (1974). *The Lost Gods of England.* NY: Oxford University Press.

Ellis-Davidson, H.R., (1964). *Gods and Myths of Northern Europe.* NY: Penguin Books.

Ellis-Davidson, H. R., (1968). *The Road to Hel.* NY: Greenwood Press.

Dubois, Thomas, (1999). *Nordic Religions in the Viking Age.* PA: University of Pennsylvania Press.

Gaiman, Neil, (1993). *American Gods.* NY: Harpertorch.

Kaldera, Raven, (2007). *Pathwalker's Guide to the Nine Worlds.* MA: Asphodel Press.

Kaldera, Raven, (2007). *Wightridden.* MA: Asphodel Press.

Kaldera, Raven, (2007). *Wyrdwalkers.* MA: Asphodel Press.

Kershaw, Kris, (2000). *The One-Eyed God.* Washington, D.C. : Journal of Indo-European Studies, Monograph No. 36.

Krasskova, Galina, (2005). *Exploring the Northern Tradition.* NJ: New Page Books.

Krasskova, Galina, (2006). *Walking Toward Yggdrasil*. MA: Asphodel Press.

Krasskova, Galina, (2006). *Sigdrifa's Prayer*. MA : Asphodel Press.

Krasskova, Galina, (2007). *Full Fathom Five: A Devotional to the Norse Gods and Goddesses of the Sea*. MA: Asphodel Press.

Krasskova, Galina, (2008). *Feeding the Flame*. MA: Asphodel Press.

MacCullough, John, (1968). *Mythology of All Races, vol. 2*. NY: Cooper Square Publisher, Inc.

Nichols, Tracy, (2007). *From the Heart, For the Heart*. MA: Asphodel Press.

Paxson, Diana, (1993). *Wodens Children Trilogy*. NY: Avon Books.

Paxson, Diana, (2005). *Taking Up the Runes*. MA: Weiser Books.

Vongvisith, Elizabeth, (2006). *Trickster, My Beloved*. MA: Asphodel Press.

Vongvisith, Elizabeth, (2007). *Love and Shadows*. MA: Asphodel Press.

Wodening, Eric, (1999). *The Threefold Initiation of Woden*. NY: Theod Press.

Young, Jean (trans.), (1954). *Prose Edda*. CA: University of California Press.

Useful Websites

http://www.cauldronfarm.com/prayerbeads/index.html#north
http: //www.odinspeaks.com
http://home.earthlink.net/-wodensharrow/
http://www.asatruringfrankfurt.de

About the Author

Rev. Galina Krasskova is a free range tribalist Heathen, and *godatheow* who has been a priest of Odin and Loki for close to fifteen years. She is the founder of Urdabrunnr Kindred in NYC, and a member of Ironwood Kindred (MA), Asatru in Frankfurt (Frankfurt am Main, Germany), and the First Kingdom Church of Asphodel (MA). Her primary interest is Heathen devotional work and she has both written and lectured extensively on this subject. Galina is heavily involved in the reconstruction of Northern Tradition shamanism and, in addition to several of her own books, has contributed extensively to Raven Kaldera's Northern Tradition Shamanism series. Galina holds a diploma in interfaith ministry from The New Seminary in NYC, a BA in religious studies from Empire State College and is currently pursuing her MA in religious studies at New York University. She is a member of the American Academy of Religion, the Religious Coalition for Reproductive Choice, and she is a staff writer for Pangaia magazine. She may be reached at urdabrunnr@yahoo.com.

Lightning Source UK Ltd.
Milton Keynes UK
UKOW02f1412180515

251752UK00001B/158/P